What others are say
a Million in a Month:

"Many chapters in Murray's book touched my soul deeply. This book isn't just for people who are interested in fund-raising. I feel that everyone could benefit from reading it."

Judith Aranow, philanthropist

"This book is sure to give energy and ideas to every fund-raiser, from beginner to experienced professional. It is filled with great advice and creativity. ... I highly recommend it."

Palmer Moe, Managing Director,
Kronkosky Charitable Foundation
San Antonio, Texas

"I enjoyed reading *How I Raised a Million in a Month* very much. It contains down-to-earth practical approaches as well as a spirit of passion, commitment, and creativity to the work in a job that most people would not want to take on. It should be a big hit!"

Morrison Heath,
attorney and foundation board member

"A delightful, clear and highly relevant guide to fund-raising."

John N. Simons, Jr.,
President & CEO, Swift & Co.

"This is a splendid guide to good fund-raising. I have been heavily involved in raising money in my community for almost 50 years. I thought I knew it all, but I got many excellent ideas from Mrs. Murray's book."

Joseph Hofheimer, Scarsdale, New York

"A precise and thoughtful overview of how to be a success-ful fund-raiser. ... Murray gives us examples of good press relations that really work and how, in the final analysis, overall positive results come from good common sense...a solid reminder of how much I've learned in my career and, even more, how much I may have forgotten. If you're in the business of fund-raising, I'd keep *How I Raised a Million in a Month* by your side always."

Sig Rogich, national political and philanthropic fund-raiser and
former advisor for U.S. Presidents
Ronald Reagan and George H.W. Bush

"Murray honestly shares her experiences—joys and even an occasional backfire—all of which contributed to her success as a motivator and fund-raiser. Her stories are life lessons that I wish I had learned thirty years ago. I could not put this remarkable book down, except when called to dinner."

Dr. Richard J. Schilling
author, artist and former hospital foundation board member

"What a magnificent personal handbook for energizing everyone who has ever endeavored to do fund-raising. ... This little book provides a practical guide to creating visibility for your organization and methods of communicating with potential donors. It should be a "must-read" for everyone involved in asking for support for nonprofit organizations.

Carol Moore, member of Association of Fund-Raising Professionals
and executive board member of Girl Scouts of Sierra Nevada

How I Raised a MILLION in a Month

*Nonprofit Fund-Raising Ideas
that Worked for Me—
and Can Work for You*

Barbara Ann Murray

Published by Cottonwood Press, Inc.
Fort Collins, Colorado
1-800-864-4297
www.cottonwoodpress.com

ISBN 1-877673-66-8

Printed in the United States of America

The names of characters in this book have been
changed, as have some physical characteristics and
descriptive details. Some of the events and characters
are composites of several individual events or per-
sons.

Illustrated by Patricia Howard

For my wonderful husband,
who encouraged me to write my heartfelt stories
about successful fund-raising.

And for all the incredible people
who made the stories possible!

Table of Contents

Introduction

When I resigned in 2003 from my position as the director of a hospital foundation, I made a leap of faith and vowed to do one last thing for the foundation: raise one million dollars in my final month on the job.

That was on November 7. By December 4, I had done it. The foundation was over a million dollars richer.

How did I raise a million dollars? My ten years in fund-raising helped set the stage, with people, experiences, and events all contributing in some way to the final month-long push to help our community. In this book, I share the stories of my years with the foundation, with the final chapter giving the details of my Million in a Month campaign.

I chose the "story" form for this book because, when we speak of matters of the heart, I think stories work best. Fund-raising *is* a matter of the heart. Yes, it does involve money and the nuts and bolts of finding that money. However, it involves so much more—the heartwarming experiences of fund-raisers, the people they help, and the people who help *them*. Stories are a powerful way of communicating to any audience. They communicate facts as well as feelings.

I don't believe anyone goes into fund-raising because they like to ask for money. Most people get involved because they believe in the cause, the organization, and their ability to help. Few enter as professionally trained fund-raisers. Like me, most come from other backgrounds and learn the art of raising money along the way.

I did my first fund-raising as a young child pulling a wagon around selling raspberries. As a high school teacher, I helped organize fund-raisers for band uniforms, athletic gear, field trips and library books. Later, as a school counselor, I helped raise money for children who needed school supplies, clothing, and even health care.

My approach to fund-raising can best be summed up by comparing it to giving a lovely dinner party. As host of the party, you decide on a guest list, prepare your entrées with great care, set a beautiful table, and then invite your guests to sit down and dine. With fund-raising, you decide on the people or groups you would like to invite to your "table" as possible donors (keeping in mind that others you don't even know might hear about it and show up, too!). You prepare your projects and programs with great care and describe the beautiful opportunities available to help others. Then you invite your guests to sit down and take advantage of that opportunity.

Fund-raising will always be a people-to-people business involving relationships and, most important, *heart*. Whether you are new to fund-raising or have been doing it for years, I hope you will find helpful ideas as well as inspiration in the stories that follow.

Barbara Ann Murray

What Happened to "Them" Might Not Happen to You

"Faith in oneself...is the best and safest course."
MICHELANGELO

I had just accepted a position as executive director of a local hospital foundation when I received word that my father, who had been suffering long and hard with cancer, had died. I jumped on a plane to make the 1000-mile trip to my hometown to say my final good-byes. My heart was heavy, and I was also feeling very anxious. My new job was to start in three days.

Family funerals can be bittersweet. While losing a loved one tears your heart out, the good part is seeing those beloved relatives that you see only at funerals and weddings. When the funeral was over, the visiting began in the basement of the church, over lunch prepared by the ladies' aid group at the church. My relatives were eager to share what had been going on in their lives. Of course, I was excited to tell them about my new position.

What I wasn't prepared for were the dismal responses to my news. People wondered why I had given up a stable job for one I didn't know anything about. One aunt shared a story about a fund-raiser she had known who developed ulcers and lasted only six months at the job. Another relative remarked, "Nobody likes people who ask for money."

My mood was going downhill fast when I spotted my favorite cousin coming into the room. I couldn't wait to talk to her and get some reassurance that I had made the right decision.

That was not to happen. Upon hearing about my job change, she all but started to cry. She told me how her best friend had taken a foundation director's position at a university, and it was the job from hell. The board members were never happy. Every department was breathing down her neck needing money. "Good heavens," she said. "Do you have any idea what you are doing???????"

Maybe I didn't. Having worked a great deal of my adult life as a high school teacher and counselor, I had never given much thought to changing careers. I liked my work with high school students. However, when I heard about the fund-raising position at the hospital, it piqued my interest. I am a firm believer in the idea that change can be good, so—with the encouragement of friends—I applied for the position.

I knew that I didn't have much experience in fund-raising, and I didn't know much about things like planned giving and annual and capital campaigns. However, I knew I had the ability to learn those skills. What I *did* have to offer was a working knowledge of the community, good leadership and organization skills, and perhaps, most important, the ability to feel comfortable with people from all walks of life. At my interview, I said that I was equally comfortable putting on a fancy dress to attend a fund-raising ball or putting on boots to meet donors in their barn.

I got the job.

On the plane returning home from the funeral, my cousin's words echoed in my brain: "Do you have any idea what you are doing?" Discouraged, I fell asleep and slept all the way back to Colorado. I awoke feeling a bit more positive. I decided that I would start my new career with an optimistic outlook, no matter what was in store for me.

What was in store for me turned out to be more than ten wonderful years filled with thousands of caring people who, together, raised millions of dollars for much-needed health programs in our community.

Years later, my cousin laughed with me many times about that dreadful conversation the day of the funeral. We learned to rejoice that what had happened to "them" in all the stories we heard did not happen to me. ■

Tips for Success:

- People have a habit of telling you worst-case scenarios. Take them with a grain of salt. What happened to someone else is not destined to happen to you.

- You know yourself better than anyone else. If a fund-raising job feels right for you, trust that feeling.

- For every bad story there is a good story. Concentrate on the good ones.

- Whether you are interviewing for a job or raising money for a project, it is important to believe in yourself and what you are doing. People give to those they believe will get the job done.

Don't Let Your Board Be Bored

"If you have zest and enthusiasm, you attract zest and enthusiasm. Life does give back in kind."
NORMAN VINCENT PEALE

What every foundation leader hopes to have is a board of directors that is fully functioning, engaged and involved. My new position came with 27 very diverse people already on board. All 27 members were asked to attend the quarterly board meetings, the first of which came up three weeks after I became the new director. I made a point of having coffee with each of the members, one at a time, so that I would at least know their names and a few things about them before the first board meeting.

The day came, and I was nervous. My packet of materials was ready, and I had note cards reminding me of names and faces. I remembered the saying, "You never get a second chance to make a first impression," and I wanted to get off to a good start. A message from a fund-raising course I had taken was also running through my head: *Your board of directors can make you or break you!*

The first meeting with my board of directors brought back memories of my many years as a high school teacher. All those new faces! I decided to try an approach I had come to value as a teacher. It always got my classes off to a great start, and I hoped it would do the same with my board.

I started by saying we all wanted the same thing: a successful experience together, and not to be *bored!* (High school students are always worried about being bored, and I suspected adults have a similar fear.) I explained that I wanted to be the very best director I could possibly be and that I had prepared a list of things the board members could count on me for. I then turned to my flip chart and went over the list:

- I would attend all meetings.

- I would always be on time.

- I would come to meetings prepared.

- I would make sure board members had what they needed to prepare for meetings, sending out information packets two weeks in advance.

- I would complete my assignments and be accountable for my responsibilities as defined in my job description.

- I would maintain a positive attitude.

- I would be a good communicator and be available when they needed me.

- I would serve as director with *pride* because I knew the work we were doing was very important.

- I would strive to represent the foundation well.

- I would have some *fun* along the way!

When I finished, I handed out paper and gave them time to write their expectations of me. I asked them to put their name and phone number on the top right corner of the paper—more tasks from my teaching days!

Finally, I handed out copies of the foundation's list of roles and responsibilities for board members. I explained that I would be calling soon to set up individual meetings to gain a better understanding of what each of their *specific* roles and responsibilities would be.

They all turned in their expectation sheets, and two members resigned. Those two said they didn't have the time needed to meet the responsibilities of a board member—a good thing to find out right away! (I was to find out later that board members who don't want to work can be a huge problem for nonprofit organizations. My list of expectations alerted the board members that they were going to be *working* board members. Many told me privately that they appreciated my bold move.) The two vacancies were filled within months by people who wanted to be a real part of this soon-to-be very active board.

At my farewell party many years later, all but two of the original 27 members were still on the board. As we reminisced, one member said that in my ten year history as director, he could never remember a meeting he didn't enjoy. He reminded everyone about my first board meeting, referring to it as the "expectations" meeting, and said that he had left that day knowing that this board would never be bored.

He was right. A board that is active and involved will never be bored. ■

Tips for Success:

- Experience counts. When appropriate, rely on what has worked for you in other situations. If you were once a teacher, try what worked in the classroom in your new position. If you were a business owner, use what you learned about marketing. If you were a stay-at-home mom, rely on the organization skills you developed in running your household. Whatever your experience, use it to your advantage.

- An *active* board is a *happy* board. Don't let board members become mere figureheads.

- Expectations are important, but everyone needs to know what they are. Make sure others know what you expect of them. Be very sure you know what they expect of *you* as well!

No Misspelled Words

*"The only real mistake is the one
from which we learn nothing."*
JOHN POWELL

It was my first formal board meeting and I had been working feverishly on what I thought was a pretty impressive packet of information to go over with board members. It was about 30 pages long and included everything from previous meeting minutes to detailed financials, budgets and objectives for the coming year.

I had been on the job as executive director of the foundation for only three months, and I had spent days, nights and weekends preparing for this meeting. "Be prepared" is a motto of mine held over from my teaching days, and it has always served me well. The more prepared you are, the more you *look* like you know what you are doing. It also makes you appear more confident, and people like that reassurance in their leader.

So I had prepared. I had read carefully all foundation packets from the past two years. I had met with each of the 27 board members individually before this meeting, putting basic information about each on a note card to help me remember details. I was ready.

I stood at the door and greeted each member by name as he or she arrived. After lunch (nothing too heavy or hard to eat), I started the formal meeting and went over the packet I had prepared. I had timed my presentation carefully so that volunteer board members could get back to their jobs. When we had discussed all the agenda items, I thanked the group for coming, and we adjourned on time. Once again I stood at the door and thanked each board member as we said our good-byes.

I was receiving lots of "Nice job," "Well done" messages as members filed out, so I was feeling pretty good about myself. Finally, the last board member approached me. He had seemed to be waiting for everyone else to leave. I smiled, referred to him by name and said "So, how do you think my first meeting went?"

I certainly wasn't prepared for his answer. He proceeded to tell me that there were *two spelling errors* in my packet! In a very nice way, he told me that he wanted nothing but success for both me and the foundation and that I should take greater care in how written materials were prepared. He reminded me that what people *see* is what they feel they will *get*.

I swallowed hard and thanked him for caring. He offered to meet me for coffee and share a few stories that might be helpful to me in my new position. I swallowed my foolish pride and took him up on the offer. As a result, I received a great deal of very helpful advice that was to serve me well in the ten years to come. ■

Tips for Success:

- Listen to what critics have to say. When it appears that someone is being critical of you, that person might really be wanting to help you to succeed.

- Take time to meet with board members one on one. Finding out about them and their expectations is very important to building a strong board. It is important to remember that board members are volunteers who need to be listened to and appreciated.

- Be open to learning from *everyone*.

Spread a Little Sunshine

"The miracle is this: the more we share,
the more we have."
PROVERB

I had been in my position as director of the foundation for only a month when I met a woman with a heart for giving and helping unlike any I had ever before encountered. In memory of her father, she wanted to do something to brighten the lives of patients while they were in the hospital.

I listened to what she had in mind. Her dream was to establish an ongoing program that would give patients "a dose of sunshine" whenever they needed it. Her sunshine program would provide a variety of items to help patients and their visitors feel better: flowers, balloons, haircuts, shampoos, videotapes, audio tapes, games, toys, books, gifts for special occasions and even meal tickets and taxi rides for family members in need of them. On holidays, she wanted to distribute personal cards and gifts to every patient in the hospital.

She had a vision of big yellow sunshine carts that could be pushed from room to room by the hospital volunteers. Best of all, all the items on the carts would be *free* to the patients!

The board and the hospital administration agreed that the sunshine carts would be a wonderful gift to the hospital. A committee was formed, big yellow carts were constructed, and hospital volunteers signed up to deliver the sunshine on a daily basis.

On every major holiday for the next ten years, the "sunshine lady" and I delivered cards, gifts and words of encouragement to every patient in the hospital. Sometimes other people would join us—nurses, doctors, administrators, board members, newspaper writers looking for a good human interest story, and even police officers, teachers and fire fighters.

Donations from the community started to arrive after a wonderful article appeared in the local newspaper about the sunshine lady and her good work. Patients and family members who had received a dose of sunshine started sending in donations. As the years went by, more big yellow sunshine carts were added for the emergency room, the pediatric unit, the cancer center, and the hospital waiting rooms.

The sunshine lady became involved in many other foundation projects as well. There was no end to the ideas she came up with for spreading sunshine. Best of all, her generosity led to generosity from others. I heard story after story from patients who wanted to share what the "sunshine" had meant to them. Many of these people later became donors to the foundation themselves. ■

Tips for Success:

- We have two ears for a reason—to *listen*.
  Great ideas are in the minds of people
  everywhere. When we are open to listening, wonderful things can happen.

- Generosity is catching. One person's generosity can lead to generosity from others.

- When we help people realize their dreams,
  they will almost certainly help us with ours.

Picnics in the House

*"It is the sweet, simple things of life
which are the real ones after all."*
LAURA INGALLS WILDER

It was a very rainy Monday morning when I called a
woman whose husband had just died, to see if she
might like to have lunch. Many memorial gifts had been
made to the foundation in his honor, and I wanted to
say "Thank you" in person and talk about how she
would like to see the memorial gifts used.

She said her favorite lunch was a picnic in the park,
but seeing that it was raining cats and dogs, she didn't
think that would be possible. Being an out-of-the-box
thinker, I suggested that I could bring a picnic lunch to
her house and we could *pretend* we were at the park.
She said she thought that sounded like a grand idea.

I arrived at noon with two picnic lunches and a
nature CD with sounds of water and birds. The

woman who answered the door was no bigger than a minute, with beautiful white hair and smiling blue eyes. She ushered me into the living room, where she had a soft-looking pink blanket opened picnic-style on the floor. We put the CD on her stereo, and our picnic began.

What also began that day was a wonderful relationship. Although she had not been involved with our foundation in the past, that was soon to change. As we ate our picnic lunches that day, she told me a lot about her husband and how he had loved the community. We started formulating plans for the best way to use the memorial gifts that so many people had made.

For over 10 years, the two of us got together many times. She was always interested in my projects and shared her ideas as well as generous donations. Because she knew so many people in the community, she also helped me meet those who could help with information, advice and, yes, money.

As the years passed, my friend lost her eyesight. Then, slowly, one physical problem after another arose. A few months before she died, I called to see how she was doing and to ask if I might stop in to see her. To

my surprise, she had a special request. She wondered if
we could have another one of those picnics on her
floor like the one we had had so many years ago.

We did, and what a time we had sitting on the pink
blanket one last time, reminiscing about all the times
we had spent together at foundation events, working
on community projects or just sitting across from one
another talking.

When she died, people told stories at her memorial
service. I found out then just how much those picnics
on the floor had meant to her. It turns out that she
had mentioned them many times to family and friends
alike. Her attorney contacted me several weeks after
the funeral to tell me that she had left the foundation a
very large gift. I smiled, looked to the heavens and said
"Thank you!" ■

Tips for Success:

- Dare to be different. Don't be afraid to think out-of-the-box and do things that are a little out of the ordinary. Most of the time, people like a change and will remember you for it.

- Building meaningful relationships is what fund-raising is all about. Although it is important to let donors know you appreciate their financial support, it is also important to get to know them for themselves. Learn to enjoy them for who they are.

The 48-Hour Rule

"Appreciation can make a day, even change a life.
Your willingness to put it into words
is all that is necessary."
MARGARET COUSINS

It has been said that the road to success is paved with gratitude. I think that is probably true for life in general, but when it comes to fund-raising, it is an absolute.

The most important rule in my foundation office was to thank our donors immediately and often. We followed the 48-hour rule very strictly. The 48-hour rule was this: For any gift received in our office, a formal acknowledgement had to be in the mail to the donor within 48 hours. If it was a first-time gift, a significant gift, or a gift from a "special" donor, a phone call had to be made within that 48-hour time frame as well.

At one of the first fund-raising conferences I attended, I heard that a donor should be thanked for every gift seven times, in seven different ways. I remember thinking that was a lot of thanking and wondered how it was possible to say thank you in seven different ways. I wanted desperately to succeed and decided that saying thank you was going to become a way of life for me.

Over the years, I found many ways to say thank you to donors. Here are some of them:

- with telephone calls.

- with formal acknowledgements on the organization's letterhead (for donor tax purposes).

- with handwritten thank-you notes, mailed with a stamp instead of metered postage. To make the thank-yous as personal as possible, I kept note cards with details about various donors, so that I wouldn't forget.

- with face-to-face meetings: home visits, meetings in my office, or over coffee or lunch.

- with public recognition—walls with donor names, plaques, lists of donor names in newsletters and news articles, for example. (It is important to remember to get the donor's permission before any kind of public recognition. Some donors like to remain anonymous.)

- with small gifts for the donors, their families, or even their pets.

- with certificates of recognition.

- with annual donor thank-you events.

- with thank-you tea parties.

- with thank-you picnics in the park.

- with an invitation to attend a board meeting for special recognition.

- by arranging for a newspaper article to be written about the donor's gift.

- by showing appreciation for the donor in other ways—remembering special occasions like birthdays and anniversaries, noticing and acknowledging things the donor and/or family members have been recognized for, sending holiday greetings, attending memorial services for loved ones, visiting them in the hospital, etc.

- by thinking creatively and taking advantage of other thank-you ideas that present themselves.

A few years ago I ran into a friend who gives often and generously to worthy causes. She told me that she had stopped donating to certain organizations because they never said thank you. She said some charities didn't return her calls, and she sometimes had trouble even getting the acknowledgment letter she needed for taxes. Her money was going to the organizations that seemed to appreciate it. As I walked to my car, I thought to myself, "The road to success *is* indeed paved with gratitude." ■

Tips for Success:

- Start and end every communication with donors with a thank you.

- Say thank you often and immediately!

Chocolate Shake and French Fries

"Well done is better than well said."
BEN FRANKLIN

When one of my board members suggested I take a potential donor to lunch (I learned early on that food and fund-raising go hand-in-hand), I made reservations at the best restaurant in town, gathered up an impressive folder filled with information about the many projects and programs our organization funded, and off I went, feeling prepared and confident.

I arrived a little early, dressed nicely and smelling good, and the prospective donor appeared shortly thereafter. We greeted each other, took our seats, and proceeded to make small talk to break the ice. Our waiter brought an impressive-looking menu, but my guest ordered only soup. Then I brought out the folder

I had so carefully put together and started talking about my organization and all its worthy projects and programs.

Our food was served, and still I talked on and on. At the end of our luncheon, I asked if my guest had any questions. Her reply really took me by surprise. She told me that she thought our foundation should use its money for projects and programs instead of spending it on expensive restaurants. She also said that she herself would rather have had a lunch of McDonald's french fries and a chocolate shake. We walked outside and said our goodbyes. I stood there feeling rather foolish as she got into her car and drove away.

As I returned to my office, I thought about how badly I had blundered and wondered if I should forget the experience ever happened or try to fix it. Because I needed donors for my causes, I decided I should try to fix it.

After waiting long enough for her to have returned home, I nervously gave this interesting woman a call and asked if I might drop by her home for a few minutes at the end of my work day. I was surprised and happy when she said that would be fine. On my way to her home, I made a short stop and arrived at her door at about 5:15 p.m. When she answered the door, I thanked her for agreeing to see me and handed her the bag I had brought her—containing a McDonald's chocolate shake and french fries. She smiled and invited me in.

As she ate, she told me how much she appreciated the fact that I had called and stopped to talk about how *she* felt about the use of donor dollars. She said I wasn't just another "fund-raiser type." I wound up staying for hours and listening to many more interesting ideas she had for our organization. She became a very involved donor and helped fund many projects in the years to come.

And yes, when it came time, she was one of the many people who helped me raise a million in a month. ■

Tips for Success:

- When you have made a mistake, fix it rather than forget it.

- Don't assume you know what another person wants or needs. *Ask.* If you ask and then listen, people will tell you what is important to them.

Paws for a Cause

"In this world we must help one another."
ERICH FROMM

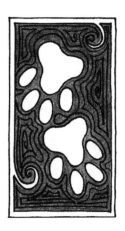

It was at the weekly lunch meeting of my local Kiwanis club that the idea first came about. The topic at our table that day turned out to be our dogs. Everyone had a dog, and everyone had a story, each funnier than the last.

As the formal meeting got under way, the topic turned to a discussion of what type of fund-raising event we should have that year. We reviewed all the events of previous years and decided to give the matter some thought and come back the next week with ideas.

As I drove back to the office, I wondered what kind of event would be different, a lot of fun, and meet our club's mission of helping children in the community. That evening, while walking my dog, I had an idea. What if our Kiwanis club and my foundation jointly sponsored an event, holding a "dog walk" to raise funds for children's health services?

I proposed the idea at the next meeting. It was one idea among many, but it got the most votes, and the planning for "Paws For A Cause" soon got underway.

As the saying goes, two heads are better than one. In this case, two organizations were better than one. Each group brought lists of sponsors, participants, helpers, and, yes, dogs to walk. The fund-raising ideas flowed. We decided that people would be asked to pay to sponsor their dogs at the event. Then there would be contests: biggest dog, smallest dog, best costume, dog/owner look-alikes, etc. We would provide snacks and beverages, and seats along the trail would be available for those who just wanted to watch the parade of dogs and owners pass by.

The result? They came in great numbers, big and little, old and young, black and white, even spotted. The dogs got out of their cars with excitement and enthusiasm to walk for a cause.

Hundreds of people showed up, too. The "Paws For A Cause" article in the newspaper the next day, along with some very cute pictures, told the story of teamwork, people and their pets, and a community working together to take care of its children.

Best of all, "Paws for a Cause" raised a lot of money. When we sat down to evaluate the event, we all agreed that we had doubled our pleasure, doubled our fun, and doubled our results. ■

Tips for Success:

- Two organizations can get twice as much accomplished in half the time. It's a win-win situation for everyone.

- Co-sponsoring events is a wonderful way to show the community that everyone benefits when organizations work together for causes.

- People *love* their pets. Pet events bring out donors who might not attend any other kind of event.

Call If You Are Lost

*"The greatest thing in this world is
not so much where we are,
but in what direction
we are moving."*
OLIVER WENDELL HOLMES

When my administrator directed me to look into
securing grant monies for some of the foundation's projects and programs, I started my research
immediately, driving to our state's research library and
spending a day perusing everything related to the
assignment. I left the library with lots of great information, the most helpful being names of books I
needed to order for my office—grant guides and how-
to books.

When the grant guides arrived, I read them carefully
and made a list of the appropriate funding sources,
matching their needs with ours. Then I prepared a plan
of action and met with the board of directors, outlin-
ing my plan and asking them for their full support. I

was pleased at their enthusiasm and went to work at once sending out letters to the appropriate funders, asking for permission to submit proposals. In the following months, I received only one request for proposal (RFP). This organization funded projects like the one we were going to be starting, and our foundation appeared similar in nature to others that had received grant monies from the organization. I thought we were a good fit.

The instructions for writing the proposal were long and complicated. I had very little experience in grant writing, but I felt I could figure it all out. I read and re-read the instructions and the many questions I needed to answer. On more than one occasion, I supplied the information I *thought* they were asking for, with a nagging feeling I might be falling short of the mark. I worked on this proposal for months and months, even taking it home nights and weekends to make sure I would get it finished in time to meet the deadline.

Finally, with the proposal due in just days, I called the organization for overnight mail instructions. The woman who answered the phone gave me the information I needed and then went on to say she wanted to go over the list of information the organization wanted, to make sure I had included everything in my proposal. "Many proposals get thrown out because they lack this or that," she said. She started on the list, and my heart sank. Some of the items I had *thought* they wanted were not what they wanted at all. I tried to make a case for a time extension to complete several items that I had done incorrectly because I had not understood the questions. The woman said that would not be possible.

I learned two important pieces of information during that conversation: (1) There is no room for "guessing" or "assuming" in grant work. Pretending to know and proceeding with incorrect information can have disastrous results. (2) I could apply again in four months.

I did submit the proposal again four months later, and while I was rewriting it, I called the woman I had talked to many times—whenever I was a little lost. I wanted to be very sure I was giving them the material they were looking for.

And yes, in the end, we did receive the grant award. ■

Tips for Success:

- Guessing and assuming don't get the job done. Facts are what is needed.

- Calling for more information does not show weakness. It shows you can be counted on to do a job and do it right.

- When you need to know something, go directly to the source of information. Asking the wrong people is often little more than guessing.

- Call as soon as you know you are lost. Time is money!

Plant Together, Grow Together

"Someone's sitting in the shade today because someone planted a tree a long time ago."
WARREN BUFFETT

W e were trying to get a wellness/nature walk project started at our hospital. It was to be a one-mile trail around the hospital campus, designed to provide a beautiful, healthy place for patients, employees, and community residents to walk. It was also to be a garden where community members could honor and remember loved ones through the purchase of plants, trees, benches, or sculpture. What existed was a one-mile cement sidewalk around the hospital campus—and a vision of what it might become.

Not having any expertise in designing trails or walks, I went to the forestry department of a nearby university for help. The professor thought it was an interesting project and said he would be willing to make the design of the trail a class project for his graduate students.

Several months later, he presented us with a unique plan. To make the trail both interesting and educational, the students had incorporated the six ecosystems found in our state into the design. They were so anxious to see their work come to life that they had even agreed to come and help plant all the trees, shrubs, plants and flowers listed on their plan.

I went to a local nursery to see what the cost of materials was going to be. The owner found the project very interesting and offered to donate a few of the items and sell the rest to us at a discount. Still, it was going to be a costly project. We were going to need a good fund-raising event.

At a gathering a few days later, an idea for an event started to take shape. A science teacher in the group said he thought an ecosystem trail of this nature would make a great outdoor lab for the entire school system to use. He thought that science students, K-12, could help the college students plant the trail and that it would be a great learning experience for everyone.

As it turned out, *all* the school's science departments wanted to be involved, as did the Girl Scouts and Boy Scouts, the 4-H clubs, and even the children's day-care center on the hospital campus. Everyone loved the idea that children would be learning about ecosystems and about planting trees, shrubs, plants and flowers. All of a sudden, we had class projects everywhere. Now what we needed was adults to oversee and help the students do the work—and *money* for everything we were going to plant.

I asked the local newspaper to run a story on the project. After all, the trail would be for the entire community to enjoy, and our own children would be doing the planting. It would also be the first and only trail of its kind in the state. The article got an overwhelming response. Hundreds of families signed up to help their kids plant, and they were all more than happy to pay an entry fee to participate. The materials were ordered, and on Arbor Day the Wellness/Nature Ecosystem Trail became a reality.

The story didn't end there. The families also wanted benches, lighting, wastebaskets, and signage to mark every item planted, and they were willing to donate the money needed to get the job done. Finally, we had *another* fund-raising event. "Art on the Walk" featured artwork created and donated by children and local artists. By selling the art at the "Art on the Walk" event, we raised money to maintain the trail for years to come.

Today the trail has grown and is a very busy place. Schools, the Scouts and the 4-H clubs all use it as their outdoor teaching lab. Hospital employees and guests walk it daily to get exercise and fresh air, and families come to see how the plants their children planted are growing. ■

Tips for Success:

- Projects that involve children are interesting to the news media. If you notify local newspapers, radio and television stations, you are likely to get a story. Those stories are free advertising for your organization, the project and the event.

- When children and families are personally involved in a project, chances are good that participants will become annual donors as well.

- Involving children and families in fundraising events helps get visibility for both the project itself and your organization—while at the same time raising money to fund the project. Here are just a few ideas for fundraising events involving children:

  Pet walks. (People pay an entry fee to show off their pets and compete for prizes donated by merchants.)

Bike and buggy parades. (Again, entrants pay a fee to participate and compete for prizes.)

Children's lawn-raking weekend. (Children volunteer their services, in return for donations to the cause.)

Children's art sales. (Children donate artwork they have created, to be sold at an auction to benefit a charity.)

Children's tournaments. (The charity sponsors a tournament—golf, tennis, swimming, softball, etc.— and the entry fees become a charity donation.)

Bike rides. (People pay to participate, with merchants donating T-shirts, food, etc.)

Walk-a-Thons. (Participants find sponsors to donate money for each mile walked.)

Car washes. (Children volunteer their services for a car wash, with people paying with a donation to the cause.)

Extra! Extra!
Read all about it!

"Without publicity there can be no public support, and without public support every nation must decay."
BENJAMIN DISRAELI

Many people have the attitude that, "If it's in the news, it must be so." That's why it's a good idea to get the good news about your organization in print as often as possible.

In my ten years with the foundation, our projects and programs were mentioned in our daily newspaper hundreds of times. They weren't all front page articles, but they were all large enough to be noticed—and getting noticed is what fund-raising is all about.

Here are some tips that I found helpful for receiving local news coverage:

- Do some research on your local newspapers. (Don't forget weekly and free publications.) Who are the decision makers? What kind of relationships have they had with your organization, or its members? Should you try to build on that relationship or improve it? What are the newspaper's policies and procedures?

- Different reporters handle different kinds of information. Find out which reporters handle stories about your area of concern. Then set up a meeting, or meetings, and get to know them. (Don't waste their time, or you may do more harm than good. Just ask to stop by to introduce yourself, or to drop by materials about your organization. Or offer to meet over a quick cup of coffee.)

- Ask your board members if they have any "ins" with reporters. Personal contacts *do* make a difference when it comes to getting your news in the news.

- Look for many different approaches to getting your information out to the public. Human interest stories are often most effective. Who has benefited from your project or program? Tell their story. Who has been a loyal volunteer, doing work for your organization? A story about that person's work will also tell the story of your organization.

- Try to find businesses who will sponsor advertising for your organization. (Newspapers really appreciate it when you *buy* space sometimes, too!) For example, every year the real estate agents in our town would take out a full-page ad listing the names of all the people who had given to the community health center through the Realtors for Kids program. This advertisement cost thousands of dollars, but the agencies divided up the bill so that each only had to pay around $200.

- People read letters to the editor. When you need more coverage for your campaigns, call people of influence in the community and ask them to write letters for you. (You can even write sample letters to help the process along.) Ask people from all walks of life so that you have mass appeal with these letters—i.e. ministers, farmers, local business people, doctors, school personnel, children, politicians, heads of other charities, and people who *need* the services.

- Find someone to write a guest editorial for you. Next to the front page headlines and the obituaries, opinion columns are often the most widely read section of local newspapers.

- Keep press releases short and to the point. Never forget to include a contact phone number so that the reporter can easily reach you for more information.

- Encourage another agency in town (like United Way, for example) to send out a press release pointing out how your organizations work together to get thing done for the community. Or suggest that a reporter interview a representative from another agency about how your groups work together.

- Don't forget sources other than your local newspaper, radio station, or television station. Find out about newsletters produced by businesses, service organizations, churches, schools, other nonprofits, and community organizations. These publications reach hundreds of people you might otherwise miss. They will often print your entire press release just as you wrote it, particularly if your first paragraph includes an angle that will appeal to their readers.

- Be creative. Never stop looking for opportunities to tell your good news to the public! ∎

The Bow on the Building

*"Never doubt that a small group of thoughtful,
committed citizens can change the world.
Indeed, it is the only thing that ever has."*
MARGARET MEAD

I t was a bitter cold December morning. The police
had sealed off the street in front of a large down-
town building, and the city's power and light department truck had just pulled up, equipped with the extension arm and bucket. About 150 people stood in front
of the building, all bundled up in warm coats and hats,
waiting for the event to begin.

With a microphone in my hand, I thanked everyone
for coming and explained that we were about to kick
off a big campaign that would bring a much needed
community health center to our city. To remind
passers-by what a great gift this center would be for
the community, and because it was the season for giving, we were placing an enormous red bow (donated

by a local florist) on the building that was to become the community health center.

We then turned our attention to the man in the power and light bucket, which was swaying in the wind 30 feet above us. We watched him carefully attach a huge red bow to the front of the building. The local newspaper photographer was there taking shots. He mentioned that he had never seen a building wrapped like a holiday package before. Neither had anyone else!

I spoke to the crowd, explaining that the clock was ticking on end-of-the-year giving and that the foundation hoped community members would open their hearts and their pocketbooks and give our community a gift it desperately needed—a community health center. We hoped that, as people drove past the building on main street, the big red bow would remind them that it was the season for giving.

The bow hanging story, complete with great pictures, appeared that night on the front page of the newspaper. My phone starting ringing off the hook with people wanting to know where they could send checks.

With the gifts came comments and stories. The comments were about how the bow was really an attention getter, a constant reminder of the help that was needed. The stories were about real people in need of health care. It seemed as though everyone knew someone who would benefit from this new center.

The bow hung on the building for almost a year. Then the center opened, and hundreds of people came for the grand opening. When the center had just completed its first year of service, it was nominated for the best community project in the state serving the medically underserved. It was referred to as the "Bow on the Building Project." I was thrilled to attend the big awards event at the state capitol. I was even more thrilled when I was called to the stage to receive the award of first place for our project. ■

Tips for Success:

- Fund-raisers are constantly looking for ways to drum up interest for the programs and projects they fund. Doing something unusual can pique people's interest and help get the job done.

- When you can tie your event to something *visually* interesting, you increase the likelihood of newspaper photos or television coverage.

- News coverage is a great help in fund-raising, but news organizations need an angle. Sometimes doing something unusual can provide just the angle needed for an interesting story.

Letter from the Lawyer

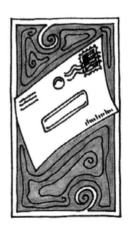

*"Turn your stumbling blocks
into stepping stones"*
ANONYMOUS

T housands of nonprofits raise millions of dollars
every year through the mail. Direct mail as a fund-
raising tool can raise money, increase your donor base,
and inform the community about your organization's
work.

I started using direct mail as a fund-raising tool early
in my career because it was fairly easy to do. First you
start with a mailing list, checking to be sure it doesn't
include the names of any deceased people. (Most charitable organizations keep an obituary file. Someone
reads the obituary pages in local newspapers every day
and enters the names into a data base. Then, when it's
time to do a mailing, you can crosscheck this list with
any other lists and eliminate these names.) Next you

add a very personal appeal letter, perhaps written by someone who benefits from your program. The letter should be interesting, short, easy to read, and written with lots of heart. Include in the mailing a brochure or written information about the project you are raising money for, a donor information card and a self-addressed postage paid return envelope.

It sounds easy, and it is. However, the problem lies in getting people to open the envelope and read your letter. The first couple of direct mailings I did for the foundation got the expected result—donations from between 0.4% and 2% of the number of people who received letters. For a few years, I did the four direct mailings a year that the foundation expected, and I got the expected results. (Every now and then you do get lucky with direct mail. One new donor sent us a check for $25,000!)

Then I got a bright idea. If the big problem with direct mail is getting people to open the mail and read it, what if I asked my board members to use their business or personal letterhead and return address envelopes for the mailing? Wasn't it worth a try?

The fact that the board members were from every walk of life really added to the possibility that my idea could work. I could divide up my direct mail list (usually about 30,000 names), and each board member would have around 1,000 names.

The 27 board members wanted our success as much as I did. To my surprise, they liked the idea so much that they even said *they* would write the appeal letters. All I would have to do was make sure that letters and envelopes matched, add the other parts of the mailing, and get everything to the post office to mail. We agreed that we would get started at once, and we set a one-month deadline for completion of the task.

It was a sight to behold—letters and envelopes from small business owners, large business leaders and employees, hospital employees, real estate agents, retired people, a veterinarian, a minister and a lawyer, all asking for donations. A group of volunteers from the hospital helped me assemble the packets, and we were extremely careful to match up letters and envelopes. It was fun to try a new way of doing the mailings, and we were very anxious to see what would happen!

It seemed we had hit on a great idea. Within a week, I started receiving envelopes with checks. We were getting a better response to the direct mailing than ever before. The return envelopes kept coming in.

Then I received a telephone call. The woman on the phone was outraged. She was so upset that I could hardly understand what she was trying to tell me. It turned out that she had received one of our letters—a letter that happened to be from a lawyer. When she calmed down, she explained that her son had been in a lot of trouble with the law, and she thought the letter from the lawyer was notification of more trouble! She went on to tell me how her heart pounded almost out of her chest as she opened the letter. She asked me how I could do such a terrible thing to people, and didn't I know how upsetting letters from lawyers were?

I apologized, apologized, and then apologized some more. I had been feeling so proud of my idea that I had failed to think about all the consequences. As it turned out, she was not the only person who didn't like receiving a letter from a lawyer. Needless to say, I never made that mistake again! We continued the program, using letters from bankers, physicians, small and large business owners, real estate agents, ministers, veterinarians, financial planners, nurses, politicians, writers, reporters, and others.

But we left out, always, the lawyers. ■

Tips for Success:

- Get feedback on a new idea. If possible, try it out on a small sample first.

- Remember that everyone makes mistakes. Learn from yours, but keep on going!

Howdy, Partner!

"Alone we can do so little;
together we can do so much."
HELEN KELLER

When I answered my phone one day, it was the beginning of fund-raising magic. The gentleman on the line turned out to be a real estate agent in town who had just read a direct mail letter I had sent to all the businesses in our community, telling them about our new community health center. In this letter, I had made a special appeal for help in meeting the health care needs of a great number of children in the community. I reminded everyone that our community had many families that were having a hard time making ends meet, often having to choose food and shelter over medical and dental care for the family.

The real estate agent told me he had been looking for some way to help local kids on a regular basis.

After reading my letter, he saw an opportunity and wanted to take action. "Do you want to 'partner'?" he asked.

I listened carefully to his thoughts about helping both children and real estate agents at the same time, about how it could be a win-win situation for both. The real estate agents would receive positive publicity for giving back to the community, and the health center would benefit by receiving both donations and publicity. We agreed to pursue a partnership, if each of our respective boards approved.

They did. The hospital foundation and the Board of Realtors both embraced the idea.

Talk about success…This partnership took off immediately. The beauty of it for me was that the real estate agents did much of the work and paid for all of the advertising. They helped publicize the center and its needs with letters, ads and articles in the newspaper, and bumper stickers and coffee mugs. Best of all, with every real estate sale, they made a donation for children to the community health center, in honor of the customer. The foundation sent each honoree a "You've been honored by your Realtor" letter. The let-

ter told about the Realtors for Kids™ program, about
the community health center and about the needs of
the children. It was surprising to see how many hon-
orees went on to make gifts of their own. I also
received many calls asking which real estate agents
were in the program because people wanted to use
them when selling or buying a house.

The program was very popular, and soon other
businesses involved in real estate transactions added
gifts. Mortgage lenders, title companies, inspectors,
appraisers, insurance companies and warranty companies all got involved with helping children through
Realtors for Kids™.

The partnership program addressed one of the
most difficult problems charitable organizations face.
It is one thing to raise start-up dollars to get a project
off the ground. It is an entirely different challenge to
maintain those projects year after year. Finding ways to
round up large numbers of givers and encourage them
to stay connected to a particular project for the long
haul takes a great deal of creative thinking. The partnership program between the real estate agents and the
foundation provided funds to maintain important pro-

grams for children in our community on an ongoing basis.

A couple of years into the program, the real estate agents added an annual softball tournament to the program and raised thousands the very first year. As I accepted the check for the foundation, I was reminded, once again, of the magic that can happen when people join hands to do good! ■

Tips for Success:

- It is essential to receive the approval and support of all concerned before embarking on any kind of partnership project. Put your agreement or understanding in writing.

- Keep communication tight between the partnership organizations. Go to each other's meetings. Give presentations to each other.

- Use a partnership program not only to raise funds but also to help you get the word out about your organization and its programs.

Mum's the Word

*"Everything becomes a little different
as soon as it is spoken out loud."*
HERMANN HESSE

My first big capital fund-raising campaign had
just gotten underway. I was excited to receive a
call from one of my board members, who told me a
meeting was being arranged with me, the board member and prospective donors to our new project. I was
to come prepared to do an in-depth presentation on
the project, including needs assessment, budgets, time-
lines, feasibility study and fund-raising analysis. I went
to work immediately. A substantial lead gift was in the
making, and I needed my presentation to be flawless.

The meeting went well—very well. Two days later, I
was called to the hospital administrator's office. When
I arrived, the board member and the donors' attorney
were already seated. The attorney announced to the

group that the donors would be making a substantial lead gift to the project. We were advised that the foundation would receive it within a few weeks.

I floated back down the hall to my office. It was news too wonderful to keep to myself, and I didn't! To my future regret, I called a few members of the capital campaign committee to tell them about this incredible gift.

It was at my home on the following Sunday evening that I received a telephone call from the board member, and it was not a pleasant call. I was informed that the donors had been at a gathering that afternoon when another guest at the event thanked them for their generous lead gift to our campaign. I was told that the donors were very surprised and unhappy that the word was out, and that I needed to call them at their home at once.

I felt embarrassed, foolish, regretful…and scared to death. I made the call, apologized, and even shed a few tears. The donors explained that they had hoped *they* could be the ones announcing their gift. I apologized some more and then asked if they would like to be guests at our board meeting the next week, so that they could make the announcement. I even asked if they would like me to get our local newspaper to cover the story. I got lucky. They liked both ideas.

The board meeting the next week was a great success. The donors got to take front and center stage to make *their* announcement, which was also front page news that evening.

I had learned a very important lesson: When it comes to donor gifts, unless you have been instructed to make the announcement, mum's the word. ■

Tips for Success:

- Confidentiality is key when it comes to fund-raising. With their first gift, let new donors know they will be receiving a permission slip (with a self-addressed, stamped envelope) on which they can indicate "yes" or "no" to receiving public acknowledgement of their gifts. Never use their names on thank-you plaques, news releases or any other materials unless you have their express permission.

- Be careful what you say, and to whom. Some donors don't want their gift mentioned to anyone at all. Others want the pleasure of being able to announce their gift themselves, and in the way they want to announce it.

The Tooth Fairy

"From small beginnings come great things."
PROVERB

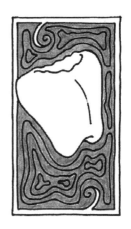

Most donations are sent by check through the mail, but this donor showed up in person, wearing blue jeans, sweat shirt and tennis shoes. She was only four years old.

She stood in the doorway to my office, clutching a baggie containing 27 crumpled-up one-dollar bills with one hand and her mother's hand with the other. The young lady explained to me that she had saved some money, and she wanted to give it to poor kids so they could get their teeth fixed. The money came from the tooth fairy, her weekly allowance, and what she had earned for picking up toys and making her bed.

I was very moved by the spirit of this little girl. I thanked her and asked her if she might like to see the clinic where her money would be used to help children get their teeth fixed. She and her mother really liked that idea, and a time was set for the following week.

I thought others would be interested in this human interest story, so I gave our newspaper a call and invited a reporter to join us. I also arranged for the dentist at the clinic to join us so that our little benefactor could also have a tour of the facility from the person in charge. The last item on my list was a thank-you plaque with our young donor's name on it, so she would have something to take home to commemorate her gift. As it turned out, she would have more than the plaque to remember that day.

The little girl and her mother showed up at the clinic, along with the dentist, a newspaper reporter, and a photographer. When the reporter asked the girl how she had found out about children needing help getting their teeth fixed, she said that she had heard her mom reading a letter she received in the mail. (That turned out to be the direct mail letter I had sent out to everyone in the community.) As she listened to her mom and dad talk about the kids needing help, she had decided that *she* could help, too!

The next day the little girl's picture was on the front page of the evening newspaper. What a surprise it was for me to get a flurry of donations from folks throughout the community who had been motivated to help when they read the news article. People called, wrote, and just showed up with messages like, "Well, if a four-year-old can give her entire savings to help children in need, then I guess I can help, too."

Four months later when the foundation had its annual donor recognition event, this little girl joined me on the stage to accept an outstanding citizen award. She received a standing ovation from over 400 people. What really put the frosting on the cake was when I gave her the microphone so she could speak to the audience. What she said was, "Did all of *you guys* give your money, too???" That brought down the house.

That wasn't the only time when the generosity of children inspired giving in others. On another occasion, three children, ages ranging from four to six, donated to the children's department of the community health center, using money they had raised selling lemonade. Again, I called the newspaper, and a won-

derful article appeared, complete with a picture showing the little girl handing me a bag of pennies. The
caption read, "Every penny counts."

A woman in the community saw the article and
decided she could help the sick children, too. She
made a gift of $10,000 to the health center, in honor
of the children who had raised money selling lemonade. ■

Tips for Success:

- When out-of-the-ordinary situations come up, drop everything and make the very most of them. Fund-raising is about people, their good hearts, and their good intentions.

- Be on the lookout for newsworthy events that can draw attention to your projects and programs. Human interest stories are one of the most effective ways to get your message across. Tell real-life stories, whether through mail solicitations, newsletters, or newspaper articles. Stories about children always receive the most response.

- "Hero" stories, especially when they involve children, are wonderful motivators for adults.

You Noticed!

*"What we do today, right now, will have
an accumulated effect on all
our tomorrows."*
ALEXANDRA STODDARD

F und-raising is first and foremost a "people" business. There are a lot of great causes for people to
choose from when it comes to charitable donations.
Finding a way to build strong, caring relationships with
donors is critical to success. The reputation of an
organization and the popularity of its programs and
projects are part of the equation, but it is person-to-
person contact that cements the relationship.

Reading the *New York Times* to see what is happen-
ing with the stock market is one way to spend time as
a fund-raiser. I found, however, that reading the local
newspaper was a much better use of my time. I looked
for the names of board members, donors, volunteers,
and others associated with the foundation. I searched

for any mention—an anniversary, the birth of a child
or grandchild, a death in the family, an award, or their
association with an organization or activity (other than
illegal activities, of course!). Just about any article that
mentioned a person associated with our foundation
got my attention. Then I clipped the article and sent it,
along with a card saying that I had noticed, so that the
person could have an extra copy for family or friends.
Often I also made a copy for our board meeting packet,
so board members would notice, too.

One day, after six years of this practice, I was invited
to a donor's home for coffee. This particular donor
had been giving generously to many foundation projects for the entire time I had been director. As we
chatted, I brought up the fact that I had just that
morning seen her name in the local newspaper for
work she was doing in the schools. She gave me a big
smile and said, "Well, leave it to you to always notice."
She asked me to stay seated because there was something she wanted to show me.

Returning to the kitchen, she set a large box on the
table. It was full of the cards, letters and clippings I
had sent her over the years. She said, "I have saved

them all. I have enough to wallpaper a room." She
went on to say that sometimes she got out the box and
"reviewed," and one day she even showed the box to
her children.

The years passed, and our relationship continued.
Then, when my Million in a Month campaign hit the
front page of the newspaper, she sent *me* the clipping
of the article, along with a very large donation and
words of appreciation and encouragement for my
campaign. She said she would be paying special attention to how I was doing, and she wanted me to know
that if I was a little short of my mark at the end of the
month, I should call her and she would put me over
the top!

I didn't have to call her, but when I reached my
goal, she did send me a congratulations card saying *she
had noticed.* ■

Tips for Success:

- All organizations send formal acknowledgements for gifts received, and many
  organizations also remember birthdays, holidays and times of sorrow. These are
  expected. It is doing the unexpected that
  makes people feel special.

- You can never say "Thank you" too often,
  but you can also find other ways to let
  people know that you appreciate them.
  Pay attention to what is going on in the
  lives of donors, board members, volunteers,
  and others associated with your program.
  Letting them know you noticed is one way
  to show appreciation.

- In the world of e-mails and voice mails,
  people still appreciate the personal touch.
  Handwritten messages, copies of articles
  cut from the newspaper, unique cards with
  meaningful messages—they all get
  noticed.

Blue Ribbon Winners

"Silent gratitude isn't much use to anyone."
GLADYS BRONWYN STERN

A fter our foundation raised money to buy a building for a community health center, renovated it,
hired a minimal staff (many doctors from the community also volunteered their time), and opened the
doors, people in need rushed in. By the end of the
first year, thousands of families had been served.

Then the project won an award for the best community project in the state serving the medically underserved. What an opportunity! I needed to thank the
people who had made the health center possible (there
were *thousands*), and at the same time raise a lot more
money to expand the center to meet the overwhelming
needs of the community. The wheels started turning.

After brainstorming ideas, I decided to purchase thousands of 1st place blue ribbons and large white envelopes with "Open Immediately...You've Won!" printed on the outside. Then I wrote a letter congratulating donors and explaining the award they had just won. The letters were personalized with each person's name, using a mail merge program. With each letter, I included a community health center brochure with statistics and specifics about the first year of operation, along with a few heartwarming patient stories to emphasize the importance of the work being done at the center. Then I made an appeal for more help, explaining that in order to keep up with the community's needs, we were going to have to expand the center.

What became known as the "Blue Ribbon Expansion Project" got off to a very good start. A whopping 82% of the people who received their blue ribbon in the mail sent in another donation.

Because we had won the award, we became the model project in the state. Senators and Representatives came to visit. Because we had so much community support, we were awarded ten out of the ten grant proposals we submitted that year for the project. With the added publicity we received during another grand opening for the center's Blue Ribbon Expansion, the donations came in record numbers. ∎

Tips for Success:

- When opportunity knocks, brainstorm to come up with as many ways as possible to use that opportunity.

- When you give the credit for the success of a project to the donors (not yourself or the organization), it increases their feeling of ownership for the project. When there is ownership, there is a sense of responsibility to the continued success of the project.

Stacy, the Dog

*"Do not let what you cannot do
interfere with what you can do."*
JOHN WOODEN

When our foundation's wellness/nature walk
project was getting off the ground, we needed
help. With a very small staff and more than twenty
foundation projects to fund and oversee, I needed a
very qualified volunteer to see the project through—
one with a lot of time, knowledge and energy.

I had no more than put out the call for a volunteer
when a woman pulling an oxygen tank behind her
appeared in my office. She explained that she and her
dog Stacy, who was out in the car, were there for the
job.

As we discussed the requirements of the job, I
found out that the woman, Marie, had been the head
librarian at a major university for many years and knew

many experts in the fields of horticulture, landscape design, and forestry. She definitely had the knowledge requirement for the job. Though she suffered from a progressive lung disease, it soon became apparent that she had plenty of time and energy as well. It turns out she belonged to a worldwide hiking association and, along with several tanks of oxygen, went on several major hikes every year. Her dog Stacy also had certain physical limitations—arthritis in her hips—but she went on the hikes, too.

Marie seemed like just the woman for the job and started immediately. Every day for many weeks in a row, I would look out my office window and see her and Stacy out on the trail, working with other people she had recruited to help with the project. A year or more went by under her careful eye, and the wellness/nature walk project grew and prospered.

Unfortunately, her health deteriorated over the next years. She was hospitalized many times, but each time I would go get her from her hospital bed and, with the assistance of a nurse, a wheelchair and oxygen, take her outside to inspect the entire trail, just so that she was satisfied that everything was as it should be. To the very end, this dedicated volunteer took care of her project.

As her condition worsened (as did Stacy's), Marie was no longer able to head up the wellness/nature walk project. However, her relationship with the foundation remained very strong. On home visits, I witnessed her declining health and watched in amazement as Stacy assisted her with so many tasks, despite the dog's own health problems.

Then a very significant event took place in Marie's life—Stacy died. I witnessed a very sad and difficult time for Marie.

On one of her last visits to the hospital, with blankets wrapped around her in the wheelchair, Marie and I ventured out to the trail. What a surprise it was for her to see a new tree planted on the walk with a plaque next to it that said, "In honor of our friend, we remember her beloved dog, Stacy." We even had a little memorial service, releasing a few balloons I had brought along for the occasion.

Within the year, Marie died. I placed a tree on the walk next to Stacy's tree. As it turned out, there were no living relatives, and Marie left her home and a large donation to the foundation to provide for the wellness/nature walk, the hospital library (remember, she had been a librarian), and the equipment needed to help patients suffering from lung disease. Though this energetic woman might have seemed, at first glance, to be too disabled to head up a charitable project, her energy and spirit soon erased any doubts. ■

Tips for Success:

- Be a "possibility" thinker. When people come forward to help, welcome them with an open mind and heart and give them a chance to show what they can do.

- Never underestimate the importance of the relationship between people and their pets. Show respect for that relationship. When appropriate, acknowledge it with *actions* as well as words.

A Wedding Story

"If opportunity doesn't knock,
build a door."
MILTON BERLE

I was at a meeting of the spiritual healing committee
held by the chaplain of our hospital when I learned
two very interesting things. First, I learned about the
Care Channel, a TV channel that pipes gentle music
and calming images into patients' rooms to enhance
their healing. The chaplain presented a videotape of
the program to the committee, along with testimonials
from patients and hospital employees who already
had this system working in their hospitals. The committee voted unanimously in favor of bringing the
Care Channel to our hospital. It was decided that the
foundation would be asked to raise the $8,000 needed
to make it happen.

Second, I learned that two members of our committee had just announced their upcoming marriage. They were both well known, highly respected employees of the hospital who had been involved in the health care of the community for many years. This couple had been close friends of mine for a long time, and I was thrilled at their news. Before leaving the meeting, the three of us made plans to get together that evening so I could hear more details about their wedding.

That evening, my friends told me that even though they were a more "mature" couple getting married later in life, they had decided to have a big wedding to celebrate their good fortune with family and friends. They wanted it all—the church wedding and a reception, complete with dancing. Because of my experience with foundation events, they wondered if I could help them with their wedding plans. I most eagerly said "Yes."

And plan we did! Since they both had so many family and friends, the guest list was over 500. We made arrangements for the church, the wedding party, the florist, the limo service, the reception and the band. During the search for the wedding invitation, the topic of gifts came up. The couple didn't want their wedding guests to buy them gifts, since they each already had fully equipped homes. We talked about how that message could be worded and decided that we would all give it some thought and discuss it the following week.

While out walking my dog later that night, it came to me. Instead of buying a wedding gift, why not invite guests to give a donation to the Care Channel in honor of the wedding couple? I knew how enthusiastic the couple was about the Care Channel. It seemed a perfect solution.

The couple loved the idea. We decided to put the request for donations on special little cards included with the wedding invitations.

The wedding day arrived, and the church overflowed with happy guests. The reception and dancing went on late into the night. A beautifully decorated mailbox sat on a table at the reception, and by the end of the evening it was stuffed with hundreds of envelopes. The bride and groom were thrilled when they tallied up all the generous donations and found that the fund had received over $7,000.

Three months later the Care Channel was installed in the hospital. All patients who come to the hospital now have nature images and healing music available to them, free of charge, at any time of the day or night. Near the elevator in the hospital there is a Care Channel donor wall. The list of names of gifts made in honor of this generous couple goes on and on and on! ■

Tips for Success:

- Gifts made "in honor of" someone are very popular. Look for new ways to offer "in honor of" gifts.

- If you have an idea, don't be afraid to share it and ask that it be considered.

- Look for unique opportunities. When we keep our eyes and ears open and think creatively, almost anything is possible!

Starry, Starry Night

"At my poor house look to behold this night
Earth-treading stars that make
dark heaven light."
WILLIAM SHAKESPEARE

It was a perfect evening. The weather forecaster had been right when he said it would not rain on June 28th. The black tie and tennis shoes event called "Starry, Starry Night" had been sold out for months. It was a formal dinner party in a nightclub setting, and it was outside, under the stars. Furthermore, it *honored* a star—a star benefactor to our foundation.

The grass was covered with large round tables with full-length black linen tablecloths. Each table looked elegant with sparkling crystal goblets and brilliant white china. The centerpieces on each table included fresh flowers and candles. Bars and buffet tables had been arranged at either side of the tables, and a stage with speaker system and outdoor lighting stood ready for the entertainment, which would go on throughout the evening.

The 150 guests arrived, dressed to the nines, most wearing tennis shoes to be comfortable on the grassy floor. As I welcomed them at the door and handed them programs for the evening, violins played in the background. The bar opened, and waiters dressed in tuxedos circled with trays of drinks and hors d'oeuvres. Dinner was announced, and as the guests were seated, local theater and symphony "stars" entertained.

Finally, we made a toast to the real star of the evening—an extraordinary woman who had given so much to the community. I explained that the proceeds from this event would go to the project our star had so generously supported throughout the years.

We had asked top-dollar for the tickets, and the guests had an opportunity to make additional "in honor of" gifts to pay tribute to their friend. During the entertainment intermission, we also auctioned several special items that had belonged to our honored star and had been given to us by the family for this purpose.

The sunset was breathtaking. The food was delicious. The entertainment was wonderful. As the sky turned dark, it filled with stars. We danced in honor of the real star of the evening, and, best of all, we raised a great deal of money that starry, starry night. ∎

Tips for Success:

- Obtain approval from the family before you start planning an event of this kind.

- Events that honor or remember an out-standing member of the community tend to be very successful. They get top-dollar billing and put your organization in the limelight as well.

- Financial sponsors for food, beverage, and entertainment are easier to obtain when the event is in honor of or in memory of an individual. Family members, places of employment, neighbors and close friends are all good sources of support.

- The funds that are raised at a memorial event should go to the project the honored person supported most over the years. Ask guidance from the family.

The Buddy System

*"We will surely get to our destination
if we join hands."*
AUNG SAN SUU KYI

Parents and teachers have been using the "buddy system" as a way of assuring the safety and comfort of children since, most probably, the beginning of time. I found the buddy system of great value in my foundation work as well. Providing a buddy to a new board member offered comfort and confidence and resulted in a more positive experience for everyone.

When I first started work with the foundation, it was a one-person department. There were 27 board members, most of whom had been with the foundation from its inception. Only a few foundation programs existed, and not much fund-raising had been done on a large scale. It was a time of change, as the community was growing by leaps and bounds, and so was the need for health care. The opportunities for growth in the foundation were vast and exciting.

As I got to know the board members, I learned that, like me, they had a lot to learn about fund-raising. We knew that we had a lot of health care programs to start and that we would have to raise a lot of money to get the job done. Nobody wanted to go out on their own and do fund-raising, so we put the buddy system into effect immediately. Everyone worked in pairs to talk to individuals and businesses about the foundation and its work.

Two by two, we talked to individuals and businesses about donations. Two by two, we wrote appeal letters and mailed them to the appropriate groups. Two by two, we got the job done. Together we raised over 13 million dollars and started 17 new community health care programs in the course of almost nine years.

In my ninth year with the foundation, the board decided it was time to bring in some new members. Many of the current board members were thinking about retiring and wanted to start preparing for a changing of the guard.

The call went out. We asked other board members to submit the names of community members they thought would be an asset to the foundation. Within two weeks, we had fifteen names. We formed a committee to interview the fifteen candidates and explain the roles and responsibilities of a board member. The committee members spelled out in detail the huge challenges that lay before the foundation and the demands that would be made of each member of the board.

The committee reported that all 15 candidates passed the interviews with flying colors. Certain that not all would consider the appointment, they invited all 15 to join the board. To the amazement of everyone, all 15 accepted. Instead of a board of 27, we now had a board of 42!

It was a bittersweet situation. There would now be 42 board members to help me, but where would I find the time to work with each one of them?

Once again I turned to the buddy system, teaming up experienced board members with new ones. For the next six months, each pair of buddies performed all foundation activities together. Each pair drove to meetings together, sat together, ate together, served on committees together and, in the end, raised a million in a month together! ∎

Tips for Success:

- Most people work better if they can share the task with someone.

- Two heads are better than one. Working with a buddy gets the creative juices flowing.

- Be a buddy to each pair of buddies. Be there to help them whenever they need you.

The Funders' Fair

*"It is one of the most beautiful compensations
of this life that no man can sincerely try
to help another without helping himself."*
RALPH WALDO EMERSON

I t was at a grant meeting held by a major funder in
our area that I first heard about funders' fairs. The
spokesperson explained that a funders' fair provides
private and public funders and nonprofits the opportunity to travel to one central place in order to learn
more about each other's work. The idea is that organizations need to work *together* to get their work done,
without any gaps or duplications in funding. This particular funder was looking for a volunteer to host a
funders' fair for our county, with the understanding
that there would be both technical and financial help
available from the funder.

I left that meeting and headed straight for a meeting with my administrator. I had been looking for an

opportunity to make inroads with this funder, and I theorized that if our organization agreed to host the funders' fair, it would strengthen our chances.

I was given the go-ahead and immediately called the funder to volunteer for the job. A steering committee of 15 was formed, and we invited 450 organizations to meet in round table fashion with about 50 funders from around the state.

The word was out. Our hope was that the funders' fair would provide an exceptional opportunity for non-profit organizations to meet face-to-face with representatives from the state's foundations, corporations and government funding agencies. Through the interaction, funders would learn more about the unique challenges facing nonprofit organizations, and, in turn, the funders would share their funding priorities and guidelines. The overall goal was to increase the numbers of grants and total dollar amount of the grants to local organizations.

The steering committee decided that pre-event orientation and training was a must. We hired a company that specialized in grant-writing guides to conduct orientation sessions. (Money from participant registration paid for the consultants.) We decided that all participants from nonprofits would be required to attend one of four orientation sessions that would be held in the two months prior to the event. The following would happen at these sessions:

The goals and objectives of the funders' fair would be spelled out:

- Organizations would learn how to identify which funders would be most likely to fund their programs.

- Participants would learn about proven techniques to market their programs quickly and effectively.

- Participants would learn about important procedures, protocol and etiquette for navigating at the fair.

- Participants would develop a detailed schedule for the day, with the names of funders they wanted to meet.

Over 500 people attended the event. Large round tables were set up everywhere, even outside under a big tent. The central feature of the day was the round table session. Each funder sat at an assigned table, and representatives from nonprofits rotated from table to table during the different sessions.

Each session began with the funder introducing his or her funding entity (foundation, corporation, or government agency) and its funding purposes and focus areas. Each of the 8-10 nonprofit representatives at the table then gave a 90-second overview of their organization's mission and program focus. Some exchange took place, giving nonprofits a sense of whether there was enough of a fit to move forward with a grant proposal.

A luncheon between the round table sessions allowed for informal contact between funders and nonprofits. The keynote speaker at the luncheon gave a brief overview of the issues facing the community and the role the community's nonprofits played in addressing those issues.

By the end of the event, funders and nonprofits had exchanged fresh ideas, discovered common interests, and developed the potential for strong partnerships for the future.

I will never know exactly how much the funders' fair helped other organizations, but I suspect that it helped a lot. It turned out to play a huge role in helping me when it came time for my Million in a Month campaign. ■

Tips for Success:

- Funders are always looking for organizations that see the big picture and work creatively to use resources wisely. A funders' fair can help organizations learn to help each other.

- Building strong relationships with funders is an important endeavor. Take advantage of any opportunities to meet with those who provide funding for nonprofits.

- A funders' fair can help other nonprofits in your community. In helping others, we help ourselves.

With a Little Help from My Friends

"I awoke this morning with devout thanksgiving for my friends, the old and the new."
RALPH WALDO EMERSON

O f all the great memories from my foundation years, the annual "friends" events are among my favorite. Every year, a group of 10-20 community members would put on an event to help raise money for one of the foundation projects. The event was usually a formal dinner and dance for about 200 guests, with an extensive silent auction of fabulous items donated by the local business community.

Year after year, the friends' group would come up with new themes to make each dinner dance better than the last, but new themes were becoming harder and harder to find. Change was in the air, and change turned out to be just what was needed.

We decided to call a brainstorming session to come up with new ideas. The first step for the volunteers who came was to evaluate what was and was not working, which led to the next step: coming up with ideas for what might work better. What came out of that meeting was a new event—a "family fest."

The family fest was to be a fun-filled carnival in October, a family day filled with food, fun, live entertainment, rides and prizes. The committee of 12 wonderful "friends" went to work, securing the county's new events center for the day. The friends sold space to local restaurants and business to advertise and sell their wares. They found sponsors to pay for rides, games and entertainment. Nearly a hundred volunteers from the hospital as well as all 43 foundation board members signed up to help. Beautiful colorful postcards advertising the event were delivered to families throughout the county. They were inserted in daily newspapers (free of charge), and given out at banks, medical offices, and stores—200,000 postcards in all.

The local newspaper advertised the family fest, explaining how the proceeds would help with the expansion of the community health center—a benefit to everyone in the community. Even the local radio stations got on the bandwagon and ran free daily advertisements for the event.

The day came, the weather was perfect, and over 23,000 people attended, making it the biggest "friends" event ever! ■

Tips for Success:

- Annual events are important to keep your organization visible in the community. However, find ways to make changes in the event from time to time, so that more people can attend.

- Events that include children and families can bring many new donors to your organization.

- See if you can establish a special "friends" group for your organization. A "friends'" organization can help you both physically and emotionally...as friends always do!

Double or Nothing

"This world belongs to the enthusiastic."
RALPH WALDO EMERSON

I t happens on the gambling tables of Las Vegas and at the horse racing tracks of Belmont. However, the risky business of "double or nothing" can be found in the nonprofit fund-raising world as well.

My first experience with a double or nothing challenge happened early in my fund-raising career. I had just sent out an appeal letter to every household in our community when I received an invitation to visit a recipient of my letter in her home. I gathered up charts, graphs, pictures and budgets—everything I could think of to share the details of the project with this prospective donor. Over coffee, the community member asked many questions and then put his cards on the table. A rather large donation would be made to this project if the dollars could be matched by other donations. It was a fund-raising challenge—a double or nothing deal—and I had three months to make it happen.

At a board meeting the next day, everyone seemed excited by the possibility of doubling the gift and getting it done in a hurry. I reminded the board that we couldn't ask others to give if we hadn't given ourselves. The board president said this would be a great time for everyone to get out their checkbooks.

They did. And so did their friends. And so did other people in the community. Very quickly, we matched the donation and doubled our money.

Double or nothing became, without a doubt, my favorite fund-raising tool, and I used it often. It was a fast and almost playful way of raising money. Individuals liked it, and so did granting organizations. As time went on, more and more grant proposals required matching funds. When it came time for my Million in a Month challenge, double or nothing played a key role.

■

Tips for Success:

- People respond well to challenges, risk and urgency—all ingredients of the double or nothing challenge. Challenges can draw attention to your cause.

- The "I will if you will" concept is a playful way of asking people for donations. People love to see their gift doubled.

Boards that Work

*"The welfare of each is bound up
in the welfare of all."*
HELEN KELLER

I t was my final board meeting. The foundation board
was present—all 43 members—and it was time to
say good-bye.

The board president invited other board members
to share thoughts and memories of our time together.
What I heard from those generous people that day
helped me to understand what a special working relationship we had shared for ten years. There were good
reasons why our foundation had been so successful.

Here are some of the ideas the board members
shared about our success, followed by a few hints for
making those ideas a reality:

Board members felt like family. They worked together well because they knew each other so well.

Hints:

- Hold at least two strictly social get-togethers each year to build relationships between board members.

- Include in every board meeting packet a section containing newsworthy information about board members and their families (copies of engagement announcements, newspaper articles about their activities, etc.).

- Have a "calling tree" among the board members to pass on important personal information, such as hospitalization or deaths in the family.

- Hold annual retreats to brainstorm and plan.

Board members were very proud to be a part of the foundation.

Hints :

- Work to get frequent news coverage for your projects and programs, to make the community aware of your organization's good work.

- As director, be involved in service clubs and other organizations that provide visibility and a good reputation for your organization.

Board members felt they were always treated with warmth and respect.

Hints:

- Drop whatever you are doing and be available when board members call or stop in to see you. Develop a genuine interest in their lives.

- When out in the community, always put your best face forward. (My administrator told me when I was hired that "Everyone has to like you all the time.")

- Listen, really listen, to board members and their ideas.

Board members were valued and given credit for the success of your organization.

Hint:

- Humility is a very important characteristic of a leader. When speaking about the accomplishments of your organization, always give others the credit. They will work hard to live up to their reputation.

The board never had to worry about accountability, credibility, legal, or financial problems.

Hints:

- Have an annual financial audit by a reputable organization.

- Prepare credible annual budgets and adhere to them.

- Keep impeccable financial records and reports. Give copies to the board every few months.

The board came to meetings knowing they would find materials well organized, agendas set and adhered to, plans of action well defined, and business conducted in a timely manner.

Hints:

- Board members are volunteers and have jobs and schedules of their own. Make sure all meetings start and end on time. Respect the time volunteers devote to the organization.

- Help the board stay focused on its goals and objectives. Have a working plan for getting each job done.

Give board members what they need to succeed.

Hint:

- Be sure that board members know exactly what is expected of them and have the information they need to understand those expectations. Be sure they have the support from you to help meet those expectations.

Many board members mentioned that working with the foundation had been one of the most important things they had done in their lives. They all agreed they would never forget the memories we had made together, especially with our Million in a Month campaign. ■

HOW I RAISED A MILLION IN A MONTH

How I Raised a Million in a Month

*"Luck is what happens when
preparation meets opportunity."*
LUCIUS ANNAEUS SENECA

I t is always great to end your career on a high note!
If you had asked me at the beginning of my fund-
raising career if I would be able to raise a million dollars in a month, I would have said, "You *must* be jok-
ing."

If you had asked me the same question five years
later, my answer might have been "Maybe." But in my
tenth year as a fund-raiser, I announced, "I am going
to raise a million in a month." And I *did!*

Someone once said that we are always getting
ready for what is to come. Everything we learn, every
relationship we make, every experience we have—all
can play a part when we need them. And so it was
with the Million in a Month campaign. I had been
getting ready for it all my life.

Late in 2003, I decided to step down from my position as director of the foundation. I loved my work but had decided to change hats and try something new in the fund-raising world. I wanted to leave the foundation projects in tiptop shape, but I was concerned about the expansion that was needed at the community health center. The center had been growing by leaps and bounds, serving more families than we had ever dreamed it would. I knew in my heart that it needed a big nest egg to ensure a successful operation well into the future. That's why I came up with the idea of the "Million in a Month" campaign. The need was great, and it seemed like there would never be a better time than *now!*

A Plan of Action

The first step was to develop a plan of action. Using the questions "Who? What? Where? Why? and How?" I brainstormed a list of everything I could think of that might help. In ten years of fund-raising, I had learned a great deal. I had worked with incredible people and experienced the miracles that can happen when good people work together to do great things. I knew this campaign was going to be another miracle. Ideas were popping into my mind in record number, and the excitement of the challenge gave me an abundant supply of energy.

Next I reviewed everything I could find about the basics of raising capital—important information I had gathered over the years from fund-raising courses, newsletters, seminars, workshops, and conferences. I constructed a giving chart, which would help me see exactly what it would take to accomplish my goal. Using people I had in mind for donations, as well as my past experiences raising money in the community, I projected how much I thought I might be able to raise at each donation level, and with how many donations. (See page 146 for my completed chart.)

Next I made a "must do" list. For any fund-raising campaign, there are critical items that must be completed before the campaign can begin. A very detailed plan generally takes months to prepare. Since I had only *days*, not weeks, my list was fairly brief and included the following:

1. Meet with the board of directors.

   • Obtain approval for the campaign.

SAMPLE Giving Chart

$1,000,000 Gift Chart		
Gift Range	# of Gifts	Total
$250,000	1	$250,000
$150,000	1	$150,000
$100,000	1	$100,000
$50,000	2	$100,000
$25,000	3	$75,000
$10,000	10	$100,000
$5,000	20	$100,000
$2,500	10	$25,000
$1,000	25	$25,000
Below $1,000	Many	$75,000
	Total	$1,000,000

- Obtain commitment from the board for help in soliciting gifts.
- Ask for a personal gift from each board member.

2. Write a "case statement" describing the history of the project and the current need, backed by up-to-date statistics.

3. Make a list of possible donors.

- Include new prospects and people who have given before.
- Include volunteers, businesses, service organizations, nonprofits, medical and dental organizations, religious organizations, politicians, and others.

4. Make a list of other important contacts.

- List media contacts.
- List those who might be available to give testimonials about how the community health center helped them.

5. Review the organization's readiness for the campaign.

- Is there appropriate staff support? If not, how do we get it?

- How do we find sufficient volunteer support?

6. Prepare the campaign budget.

   - What will be the fund-raising goal? Estimate the revenues to be raised with the campaign.

   - What will be the fund-raising costs? Include advertising, postage, printing, paper supplies, purchased services such as direct mail services, travel, catering, etc.

7. Make a timetable with a detailed day-to-day, hour-to-hour list of what needs to be done.

The Budget

The Million in a Month campaign was a fund-raiser I had not included in my budget, and it came almost at the end of the fiscal year. I had money left in the budget for some items that would be needed (paper and envelopes, printing, and a direct mail company's service), but the line items of postage and advertising were pretty well depleted.

An additional problem was that, because of our urgent, one-month deadline, our direct mail piece would need to arrive quickly. That meant mailing approximately 50,000 pieces first class at 50 cents each—or $25,000. I had only $2,500 left in my budget, so I definitely needed *help!*

I decided to look for sponsors to help cover the cost of this mailing. At the end of the fiscal year, businesses often have money left in *their* budgets to donate to a good community cause. I made some calls and I was able to round up all the help I needed to get the letters in the mail.

As for advertising costs? All the publicity we received for the Million in a Month campaign turned out to be free!

A Jump-start

Next came the campaign timetable, media contacts, and people. The plan was shaping up.

What I needed next was a jump-start, and I had an idea. I made a call and then headed for the office of the director of a local charitable trust. This trust had been set up by a pioneer of our community, a businessman and philanthropist of the highest order, now deceased. The trust was named in his honor. Because providing health care to the underserved in our community was one of its missions, this particular trust had shown a great deal of interest in the community health center ever since the project began.

I laid my cards on the table. If I were going to succeed in raising a million in a month, I would need a lead gift that would get the attention of the community and motivate everyone to get involved in this campaign. We talked, and we toured the community health center. Then I was invited to submit a challenge grant for $500,000 in honor and memory of the trust's namesake, with the understanding that I would have to match the money dollar for dollar with community donations—and do it all in *one month!*

I said, "Thank you, thank you, thank you"…and floated out to my car. In two hours, I had written the grant. The next day we received funding—provided we matched the money dollar for dollar in the time allotted.

Now I was ready to construct a fund-raising pyramid, a visual map to chart my course. The national model for a capital campaign recommends seeking a lead gift of 10-20% of the total goal. Because of the challenge grant, our particular fund-raising pyramid varied significantly from the national model. (See page 152 for fund-raising pyramids.)

The Board Gets on Board

At an emergency board meeting, all 43 board members agreed to roll up their sleeves and get to work. Because of the recent success of our "family fest," attended by over 23,000 community members, there was a great deal of excitement and a definite "We can do it!" enthusiasm in the air.

We decided to use the buddy system again. It had served us well in the past, and we all found working together easier and more fun than working alone. I agreed to come up with specific assignments for the board members within a few days, and they agreed that they would go to work immediately! The urgency of the *one month* challenge seemed to be working in my favor.

Something else in my favor was the fact that I had the best board president a person could ever ask for during an adventure like this one. She was very excited

Capital Campaign
National Giving Profile
($500,000 goal)

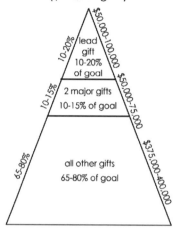

Million in a Month
Campaign Giving Profile
($500,000 matching goal)

about the campaign, and her fund-raising experience far surpassed mine. She told me she would be my "buddy" and work side by side with me every day, doing whatever was needed to get the job done.

We went to work immediately, using my timetable to set the plan into action. The timetable had four main categories:

1. Seek media coverage.

2. Complete a direct mail campaign seeking donations.

3. Make personal calls and visits.

4. Seek help from "partners."

Media Coverage

We needed to get the word out to the community, and a quick call to the local newspaper got us the media coverage we had hoped for—front page headlines announcing the challenge to the community. Many articles would follow, and all used the "Bow on the Building" symbol we had developed with the earlier campaign. Community members recognized that it stood for a project near and dear to their hearts: the community health center.

The Direct Mail Campaign

The board president went to work writing several different appeal letters designed for the various and specific professional groups our board members belonged to. The plan was that, after the letters were written, the appropriate board members would put them on their own letterhead, sign them, and enclose envelopes with their return address. We had used this technique before and (except for the letter from a lawyer!) the campaigns had been very successful.

We also needed testimonials to include in the mailing. I agreed to put in a few calls to health center patients I knew would be more than happy to tell their stories. I had learned over the years that testimonials given by the people who have been impacted by a program are a highly effective way to attract interest to the cause…and that donations always follow.

Next I made a quick stop to see the direct mail people a few blocks from my office. I had used them every time I had a large mailing to do. They were extremely dependable and would work around the clock to get an urgent mailing out. I explained that we were going to need large envelopes with the "Building with a Bow" logo, stationery with the same logo, and the names of all 43 board members running down the right margin of the paper. We would need return envelopes and coupons, *and* we were going to need enough for every household and business in our community. That meant 50,000 of everything!

The direct mail company would also do the mail merges necessary to match the different letters to the different targeted groups. Every household that wasn't on a specific list would get a "Dear Friend and Neighbor" letter. I agreed to have all the different letters signed and ready in three days. The company agreed to have the letterhead, envelopes and mail merges ready. If all went as planned, the mailing would go out in five days!

Personal Calls and Visits

I had a few more cards to play before preparing the lists of calls and visits the board members would need to make. As I said before, I had been getting ready for a long time for what I was about to do. I made three very important calls to three different people and arranged meetings with each the next morning. As it turned out, all three would offer more help than I had ever thought possible.

The first meeting was with a former board member and business leader in the community. He had read about the challenge in the newspaper and thought the campaign for the expansion of the health center was very important to the community. He had been very close friends with the founder of the trust and thought the fact that the campaign was in honor and memory of this man was very important. We reminisced about our work together, starting the center. Then he said, "Well, if we are going to do this, we had better get started." Then he took out his checkbook and wrote a check for $250,000!

I immediately called the local newspaper and arranged for a reporter to do an interview with the donor. The article in the paper the next day told the story of an outstanding community member who had just stepped up to the challenge and was encouraging everyone else to do the same. The momentum was building.

Next I met with the previous board president, who had worked with me relentlessly to get the health center started. She and her husband had lived in the community for many years and served on countless charitable boards, and they were respected throughout the community. As I explained the challenge to both of them, they offered to go to a leading developer in the area and encourage involvement in this campaign. They explained that they had worked for the grandfather and father of the developer many years before. This personal connection was key to the $150,000 gift that soon was to follow.

The third meeting that morning was with the director of a well-known community charity, a nonprofit organization that the foundation had partnered with on several occasions. Because the health center delivered primary health care to so many families that were uninsured and underserved, my request for a donation was approved, and a check for $25,000 soon arrived.

Again, the newspaper found this donation newsworthy, and we received more publicity. Community members were now fully aware of the campaign and poised to receive a letter asking for *their* help. With three weeks and two days to go in our campaign, we now were down to needing only $75,000 more to fill the requirement for the matching grant. Now we needed to return to the direct mail portion of the plan.

The board president and I met the next morning (as we would *every* morning for the next two weeks). She had all the appeal letters written, each with the same basic information but with a slightly different "slant" for each particular group. There were letters directed to each of the following groups:

- Previous donors to the community health center (They would also get a call or visit.)

- Physicians and dentists

- Churches

- Large businesses

- Small businesses

- Chamber of Commerce members

- Service clubs

- Realtors

- Bankers

- Veterinarians

- Financial planners

- Insurance agencies

- Friends and neighbors (for every household not in another category)

In addition, the president had written a specific letter to the board members, explaining the importance of their individual gifts. I added a paragraph, sharing that someone had pointed out to me that the last four letters of "enthusiasm" are *iasm,* which stands for "I am sold myself." This was a reminder that we should not ask others to do what we are not willing to do ourselves.

By now four major articles about the double or nothing challenge had appeared in the local newspaper. With the excitement growing around the challenge, it was easy to arrange for several more to follow in close fashion. After all, it was the season for giving, and the stories about a community that takes care of its own made for great reading. The articles that followed included testimonials from patients at the community health center, stories about organizations and businesses helping the cause, and updates about how the campaign was going. Key people in the community also sent letters to the editor encouraging people to help meet the challenge grant.

While all this was going on, board members were hard at work with their "call or visit" lists. Anyone who had given to the community heath center in the past received a visit. I can't say enough about how important this personal contact was to the campaign, or to any fund-raising campaign. People give to *people* who are working for causes, so the magic is in the personal contact.

Very quickly, gifts came pouring in. Some donations were in the thousands, some in the hundreds, and others were for $5.00, $10.00 or $25.00. They *all* counted toward the match.

Calling on Partners

We had many "partners" in the Million in a Month campaign—service clubs, churches, and businesses. They all helped get the word out through *their* newsletters, programs and mailings. There is power in numbers, and the number of people helping with this campaign was staggering.

Everywhere I went, I heard people talking about the Million in a Month campaign—in grocery stores, at gas stations, at the library, at the post office, at banks, at stores, and even at a bridal shower for a distant relative. People were wondering if we were going to make it, if we were really going to be able to raise a Million in a Month.

Mission Accomplished

On December 4, 2003, a few days before the month was up, the front page of our newspaper announced the results. The headlines read: "Clinic Fund Amasses $1 Million."

We had done it.

All I could say was, "Look what can happen when good people come together to do great things!" ■

Parting Thoughts

"Relationships create the fabric of our lives.
They are the fibers that weave all things together."
Eden Froust

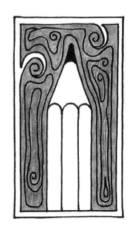

We live in a nation that cares. Last year American individuals, estates, foundations, and corporations gave an estimated $241 billion to charitable causes.* Americans have a rich history of giving and year after year demonstrate their commitment to the good works done by charities. Charities couldn't do good work if they did not have good leaders, staff and committed volunteers.

Fund-raising is not easy work, but it is noble work. In my experience, it is very *good* people who get involved with fund-raising, either as staff, volunteers, or benefactors. The programs and projects that are made possible in our communities through charitable work make our world a better place for us all.

*Giving USA 2004, a study released by Giving USA Foundation

The stories I have shared with you are my stories. You have *your* stories as well. I remind you to reflect on your stories to remind yourself of the good you are doing. Also share your stories, often, as a way to teach important life-lessons and give witness to the good in the world that takes place every day. Stories motivate people to get involved. They get to the heart-of-the-matter, where fund-raising lives.

I could never have reached my Million in a Month goal by myself. All the steps along the way, all the great people who played their part, all the stories that led up to our success—that's what allowed it to happen. When all is said and done, what happened to *me* in *my* community could happen to *you* in *your* community! I wish you well....

Barbara Ann Murray

APPENDIX

Where to Go for Up-to-Date Reports, Newsletters, Conferences, Memberships

"Know where to find the information and how to use it. That's the secret of success"

ALBERT EINSTEIN

T he following organizations provide information that is helpful to nonprofit organizations interested in fund-raising. The list is by no means exhaustive but includes groups that I found helpful in my work as director of a nonprofit hospital foundation.

American Association of Fund-raising Counsel

(AAFRC), Glenview, IL. Web: www.aafrc.org. Phone: 800-462-2372. Promotes professional, ethical, and legal standards of practice in philanthropy and advances research and education about philanthropy. Publishes *Giving USA*, an annual report on philanthropy that lists sources of funding and recipients of contributions.

The Association for Healthcare Philanthropy

(AHP), Falls Church, VA. Web: www.ahp.org. Phone: 703-532-6243. Provides updated information about fund-raising for healthcare. Members can access the AHP Resource Information Center Library, which contains information on a variety of issues regarding healthcare philanthropy. Non-members can find useful information provided by the Library, including frequently asked questions about fund-raising and a recommended list of fund-raising books.

Association for Research on Nonprofit Organizations and Voluntary Action (ARNOVA),

Indianapolis, IN. Web: www.arnova.org. Phone: 317-684-2120. Works to strengthen the research community in the field of nonprofit and philanthropic studies. Provides nonprofit professionals with philanthropic research information, as well as a forum for exchanging ideas via annual conferences, electronic discussions, and special interest groups.

The Association of Fund-raising Professionals

(AFP), Alexandria, VA. Web: www.afpnet.org. Phone:

703-684-0410. Fosters development and growth of fund-raising professionals through training. Online and on-site Resource Center provides members with free access to reference works and periodicals on fund-raising. Non-members can pay a fee to access services.

Association of Governing Boards of Universities and Colleges, Washington, D.C. Web:

www.agb.org. Phone: 202-296-8400. Provides guidance to university and college presidents and boards. Its Foundation Consulting Service provides public university and college foundations with expertise in addressing foundation issues.

Association of Professional Researchers for Advance-ment (APRA), Naperville, IL. Web:

www.APRAhome.org. Phone: 630-717-8160. Supplies nonprofit organizations the research they need to develop successful fund-raising efforts.

BBB Wise Giving Alliance, Arlington, VA. Web:

www.give.org. Phone: 703-276-0100. Collects and distributes information on nonprofit organizations that solicit nationally or have national or international program services. When charities have been the subject of inquiries, it asks for information about their programs, governance, fund-raising practices, and finances. Publishes the quarterly BBB Wise Giving Guide to help donors make informed giving decisions.

Council for Advancement and Support of Education (CASE), Washington, D.C. Web:

www.case.org. Phone: 202-328-2273. Supports education by helping its members build stronger relationships with their alumni and donors, raise funds for campus projects, market their institutions to prospective students, diversify the profession, and foster public support of education. CASE's Commission on Philanthropy directs research to examine and evaluate professional practices.

Council on Foundations (COF), Washington,

D.C. Web: www.cof.org. Phone: 202-466-6512. Made up of more than 2,000 grant making foundations and giving programs worldwide, it provides leadership expertise, legal services, networking opportunities, and other services to its members and to the general public.

GuideStar—the National Database of Nonprofit Organizations, Williamsburg, VA. Web: www.guidestar.org. Phone: 757-229-4631. A free service with information on the programs and finances of more than a million American charities and nonprofit organizations. Publishes a free, monthly e-newsletter.

The Grantsmanship Center (TGCI), Los Angeles, CA. Web: www.tgci.com. Phone: 213-482-9860. Provides grantsmanship training, workshops, and low-cost publications to nonprofit organizations and government agencies. Also publishes resources for nonprofits and fund-raisers.

Independent Sector, Washington, D.C. Web: www.independentsector.org. Phone: 202-467-6100. A coalition of foundations, nonprofit organizations, corporations, and individuals that provides information and resources to nonprofits and works on public policy issues that relate to the nonprofit sector.

National Center for Charitable Statistics

(NCCS), Washington, D.C. Web: nccsdataweb.urban.org. Phone: 866-518-3874. The national clearinghouse of data on the nonprofit sector in the United States. Develops and disseminates high quality data on non-profit organizations and their activities for use in research.

National Committee on Planned Giving®

(NCPG), Indianapolis, IN 46225. Web: www.ncpg.org. Phone: 317-269-6274. A professional association for people whose work includes developing, marketing, and administering charitable planned gifts.

National Council of Nonprofit Associations

(NCNA), Washington, D.C. Web: www.ncna.org. Phone: 202-962-0322. A network of 39 state and regional associations of nonprofits, representing over 22,000 nonprofits. Strengthens local nonprofits by keeping them connected to national networks and the latest resources in the field.

10 Tips for Becoming
a Successful Fund-Raiser

"Act as if what you do makes a difference. It does."
WILLIAM JAMES

1. Be educated. Learn all you can about the job you are doing so you can do the best job possible.

2. Be optimistic. Work hard, and believe that most things *are* possible. Celebrate every accomplishment, large and small.

3. Be responsible. Have an "If it's going to be, it's up to me" philosophy. Show that you are accountable, reliable and dependable, in both words and actions.

4. Be honest, ethical and trustworthy. Integrity matters. (Two rules of thumb: If you don't know, find out. When in doubt, don't.)

5. Be grateful. Appreciate all the good that comes to you, whether it be in time, energy or money.

6. Be sincere. A personal belief in what you are doing is a must.

7. Be organized. Keep track of everything. If you don't have a good memory, take great notes.

8. Be creative. Think outside the box and try new ideas.

9. Be a champion for your cause. Inspire others with your enthusiasm.

10. Be selfless. Keep your eye on the cause and give the credit to others.

About the Author

Barbara Ann Murray is a former high school teacher and counselor who served as the executive director of a hospital foundation for ten years. She and her husband Garvin have five grown children.

In addition to *How I Raised a Million in a Month,* she is also the author of a series of children's books that feature her dog, Murry Murray, as the main character. She lives in Colorado with her husband and her dog and enjoys speaking to groups and giving workshops on fund-raising.